TEST-TAKING SKILLS

Written by
Elaine Troisi

Illustrated by
Buck Jones

Cover Illustration by
Barbara Friedman

Edited by
Barbara G. Hoffman

FS30207 Test-Taking Skills Grade 7
All rights reserved—Printed in the U.S.A.
Copyright © 1998 Frank Schaffer Publications, Inc.
23740 Hawthorne Blvd., Torrance, CA 90505

TEST-TAKING SKILLS

GRADE 7

Parents, students, teachers, and administrators are interested in the many forms of student assessment. Traditional assessments can take the form of the textbook test, the teacher-made test, and the standardized achievement test. The information provided by such assessments helps measure student achievement, determine student and program strengths and weaknesses, make decisions about student placement, and plan curriculum changes. Whatever their intended purpose, tests have a valued role in education.

Since tests are important measures of student achievement, students can benefit from practicing a variety of test-taking strategies. Students who remain inexperienced in test-taking strategies often earn scores that reflect test anxiety, not real learning. On the other hand, students who are comfortable with the test-taking process can earn scores that reflect their true abilities. Consequently, efforts made to increase students' comfort and skill in the test-taking process will likely have a positive impact on their test outcomes.

This resource will provide students with practice in the study skills and test-taking strategies that will increase their comfort in a variety of testing situations across the curriculum. The activities in this workbook allow students to practice answering the types of questions found in classroom and standardized tests, including essay, short answer, matching, multiple choice, and true/false questions.

The activities in this book can be used as supplemental activities to accompany almost any curriculum. The lessons are self-explanatory and self-contained, enabling your students to work independently, in collaborative groups, or as an entire class.

Key to icons:

 Time Management

 Planning

 Strategy

 Practice

FS30207 Test-Taking Skills

Review Your Textbooks

- To learn better and faster, review your textbooks. Key sections to review are listed for you.
  - Introductions that tell you what to expect
  - Lists of important terms to learn
  - **Boldface** or *italics* that highlight key words
  - Charts, graphs, maps, and illustrations
  - Questions at the end of reading passages
  - Summary sections that review important ideas

Preview questions about Guilin, China before reading the passage that follows. Note: In most cases, questions come after the reading passage, and not before.

1. Briefly explain how the mountain peaks of Guilin were formed.

2. In what way is the river important to the life of the people along the Li River?

3. Write a sentence that summarizes the main idea in the second paragraph.

Read the passage about the region near Guilin in China and highlight the important words or phrases that help you answer the questions.

Guilin, a modern city in southern China surrounded by mystical mountain peaks, lies along the Li River. Han Yu, a poet who lived a thousand years ago, wrote that "the river forms a green silk belt; the mountains are like blue jade hairpins." The pointy peaks that rise from the plain along the river are really karst formations, pushed up from a limestone seabed millions of years ago.

The people who live near the Li River reside in thatched-roof farmhouses. The river provides fish for the people to eat, as well as wet lands for farming rice. The river is also the transportation that carries children to and from school and brings farmers and their hens, pigs, and vegetables to busy cities like the modern Guilin. The river, the earth, and the people live in harmony.

Answer the questions you previewed above on the lines provided here.

1. _____

2. _____

3. _____

FS30207 Test-Taking Skills

Name _____

Just for the Record!

Use the organizer below to record your test dates and what you need to do to prepare. After each test has been graded, record your grade. The sample shows you how to use the chart. Your teacher can help you select the topics and materials you need to study.

The Subject: Math			
Topics to be covered in test	**Things I should review before the test**	**✓ each item reviewed**	**Test Score**
Test Date: April 2 place value, adding decimals, subtracting decimals	a. text pages 195-210 b. 3 decimal & place value worksheets c. practice writing numbers to the hundred millions	✓ on 3/29 ✓ on 3/30 ✓ on 3/31	

The Subject:			
Topics to be covered in test	**Things I should review before the test**	**✓ each item reviewed**	**Test Score**
Test Date:	a. b. c.		

The Subject:			
Topics to be covered in test	**Things I should review before the test**	**✓ each item reviewed**	**Test Score**
Test Date	a. b. c.		

Name _____

Be Your Own Manager

This chart will help you manage your time so that you can do things you want to do and still make the grade! **Complete the chart by writing in the exact time in hours you currently spend each day on each activity listed.**

Activities	Monday	Tuesday	Wednesday	Thursday	Friday	Saturday	Sunday
Homework							
Sports							
Clubs							
Music/Dance/Art							
Jobs/Chores							
Volunteer Work							
Television							
Telephone/Friends							
Other							

After you complete the chart, think about the different ways you spend your time. How many hours a day do you watch television? How many hours do you spend on homework? Write two ways you can improve the way you spend your time.

_____

_____

_____

Get Ready, Get Set, Get Organized!

- **Color Coordinate**

Would you wear dress shoes with your gym clothes? Probably not! You like to put clothes together in ways that make sense to you and that fill your need for comfort and style. Why not do the same with your textbooks and notebooks? With your books and notebooks color-coded, you'll be able to quickly find the information you need—by color! Here's how:

— Acquire several three-holed soft vinyl binders—a different color for each subject.

— Cover each textbook with paper that is the same color as its matching binder, or decorate a plain brown book cover with stickers to match the color of the binder.

The color_____ = _____   The color_____ = _____

The color_____ = _____   The color_____ = _____

- **Organize Each Subject Notebook**

— Insert three 3-holed pocket dividers in each vinyl binder.

— Label the pockets: **hand-outs**, **homework**, and **tests**.

— Insert a plain divider and label it **notes**.

— Fill the notebook with loose-leaf, lined notebook paper to use for your notes.

- **Use An Assignment Book**

— Get an assignment book that has spaces for you to write daily assignments by subject.

— Jot down assignments with their due dates as they are given.

— Write down any special instructions your teachers may give you.

— Mark test dates, along with a daily schedule for preparing for each test.

— Maintain a monthly assignment calendar for long term projects, complete with daily goals or steps that will help you meet those deadlines.

- **Set A Goal**

I will be organized by _____.
(date)

To accomplish this goal I need to: _____

_____

_____

_____

Name_____

Down Write Smart!

Here's how to take notes on a class lecture or an assigned reading.

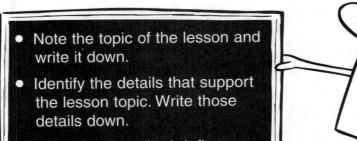

- Note the topic of the lesson and write it down.
- Identify the details that support the lesson topic. Write those details down.
- Define or describe briefly important terms or ideas.

Unless your teacher requires you to take notes in a certain style, you can choose the method that works best for you, such as the simple outline shown here.

Read the following passage and complete the outline.

During the first half of this century, there were some amazing advances in medicine. Some of them involved the invention of devices that were used to detect or treat disease. Among the devices invented early in the century was the EEG. The electroencephalogram (EEG) was first used in Germany in 1929. It allowed doctors to record the electrical activity of the brain. The EEG is still used today to help doctors diagnose various ills. Another invention early in the twentieth century was the pacemaker, which was created by A.S. Hyman in 1932. The pacemaker received much attention when it was used in 1964 to save the life of Peter Sellers, a popular actor. The pacemaker, which sends a small electric impulse into the heart to keep it beating, is still used today.

Main Idea: _____

_____

I. The Electroencephalogram (EEG)

    A. _____

    B. _____

    C. _____

II. The Pacemaker

    A. _____

    B. _____

    C. _____

FS30207 Test-Taking Skills

Name _____

Become Test Smart!

When your teacher hands you a test, should you start right away, or should you scan the test first? You might think getting started right away will help you finish on time, but by rushing to begin, you might actually find yourself with too little time to answer every question. The solution?

- Scan the test.

- Listen to your teacher's explanations.

- Check to see how many points each section is worth.

- Make a time schedule for completing each section and stick to it.

Example: A science test has 42 questions and is worth a total of 100 points. You must complete the test in 40 minutes. In the space provided below, indicate the amount of time you would spend on each section. One section has been filled in for you.

_____ Scan the test

5 minutes 10 points for ten *matching* questions

_____ 20 points for ten *fill-in-the-blank* questions

_____ 20 points for ten *short-answer* questions

_____ 20 points for ten *multiple-choice* questions

_____ 30 points for two *essay* questions

_____ Review work

_____ **Total time**

- Read all the directions before you begin.
  Some directions are simple; others are more complex. So, before you start a test, be sure to carefully read all the directions!

Read the following directions and underline key words.

Key words are words that explain the task. The first set has been done for you.

Directions for an English test: Cross out the misspelled words. Then write the correct spelling above each misspelled word. Finally, insert commas in the sentences where needed.

Directions for a math test: Read each word problem carefully. Write the name of the process you must use to solve it. Solve the problem. Show your work. Circle the final solution.

Directions for a science test: Select two constellations from the list and draw them. Briefly explain the legend that accompanies the name of just one of the constellations you drew.

Directions for a history test: Read each statement. Write **T** if it is true, or write **F** if it is false. Then, rewrite each false statement to make it true.

Directions for a reading test: Read the passage carefully. Select the answer that best identifies its main idea. Record your answers on the answer sheet.

Name_____

Goodbye, Test Stress!

Taking a test can be a lot like playing a soccer game or performing a musical piece at a piano recital. Just as your emotions can help or hurt your during a game or event, they can help or hurt you during a test. A feeling of anticipation can increase your alertness and improve your performance. However, feeling too much stress can distract you and hurt your test performance. Therefore, it is important to control your stress level while taking a test.

- Know when a test will be given.
- Make time to study for the test.
- Get plenty of rest before the test.
- Eat nutritious food to fuel your brain and body.

Answer the following questions. Plan a strategy to reduce stress at the time of your next test.

_____

1. What is the date and subject of your next test? Be specific. For example, is it a history test on World War II? Is it a math test on dividing mixed numbers?

_____

2. What is your study plan? Be specific. What days will you study? What times will you study? Where will you study?

_____

_____

_____

_____

3. To be alert and ready to do your best, it is important to be well rested. How many hours of sleep do you need each night to feel well rested? _____

   To be completely rested, what time will you need to go to bed the night before the test?

_____

4. For your body to do its best, you need to eat a healthy and balanced diet. What will you have for breakfast on test day? If the test is in the afternoon, what will you have for lunch that day?

_____

_____

FS30207 Test-Taking Skills

Name _____

The Match Maker

Many tests include matching questions. The directions may state that you should match, for example, definitions with terms, authors with books, or dates with events. Even a math test can include matching questions.

- Predict the answer to locate the match more quickly.

Complete the following matching test.

_____ 1. a four-sided shape   a. pentagon

_____ 2. a three-sided shape   b. octagon

_____ 3. a five-sided shape   c. decagon

_____ 4. an eight-sided shape   d. quadrilateral

_____ 5. a ten-sided shape   e. triangle

- Make flash cards to review the terms or events you are expected to know for the test. Write one term on one side and its matching definition on the other side. As you study, shuffle the cards often so that you are not using them in the same order. Have a partner test you using the flash cards.

Use a dictionary to find the definitions and examples for the words listed below. Make flash cards.

simile   metaphor   onomatopoeia   alliteration

Work with a partner to practice these literary terms and their definitions. Take turns. Mix up the cards. Work until you feel confident to take the following matching test.

Look at the term and think of its definition. Apply what you know to find the correct match.

Match the term with its example.

_____ 6. simile   f. With a loud crack, the lightning split the tree.

_____ 7. metaphor   g. Daniel dangled in the deep dark ditch 'til dawn, waiting for rescue.

_____ 8. onomatopoeia   h. With nerves of steel, the fireman made the daring rooftop rescue.

_____ 9. alliteration   i. The teacher's explanation was as clear as crystal.

Is It True? Or Is It False?

It's important to pay careful attention to the wording of true/false test questions. Some questions include words that change the sentence's meaning.

- Some words are clues that you should select false as the answer. They do not allow room for debate or exception, and include the words **always**, **all**, **every**, **none**, **never**, **best**, and **worst**.

Example: False   All teenagers are disrespectful.

In the above example, the word **all** is the clue word. Is the statement true of **all** teens? Perhaps some teens are disrespectful, but certainly not all.

- Other words are clues that you should select true as the answer, such as **sometimes**, **some**, **many**, **most**, **often**, **generally**, **frequently**, and **usually**. These words allow room for debate or exception.

Examine the following true/false questions. Underline the clue words. On the line, write the answer to the problem, T for True, F for False.

_____ 1. The writers of the Declaration of Independence were always in full agreement.

_____ 2. All creatures in the sea are fish.

_____ 3. Most children of the United States are immunized against polio.

_____ 4. The value of the American dollar always remains exactly the same everywhere in the world.

_____ 5. Carpet is the most durable and least expensive form of floor covering.

_____ 6. Many children across the United States are likely to go to summer camp this year.

_____ 7. All living things are made of countless cells.

Pick two of the above statements which are false. Rewrite them in the space below to make them true.

_____

_____

_____

_____

_____

More Words of Truth About True and False

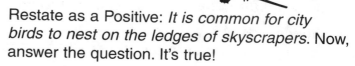

- Some tests include true/false questions containing double negatives. A double negative is two negative words placed together in a sentence. It is also a combination of a negative word with a word with a negative prefix.

Negative words are: **never   not   no   none   nor   neither**

Negative prefixes: **dis-   in-   non-   un-   im-   mis-**

The example below shows you how to restate a double negative true/false statement.

Negative: It is <u>not</u> uncommon for city birds to nest on ledges of skyscrapers.

Restate as a Positive: *It is common for city birds to nest on the ledges of skyscrapers*. Now, answer the question. It's true!

Cross out the negative words and prefixes in the following questions. Rewrite each as a positive statement on the line below it. Finally, answer the question by writing T or F.

_____ 1. During severe tornados, it is not impossible for entire buildings to be lifted off their foundations.

_____

_____ 2. Excellent athletes were not unknown in Ancient Greece.

_____

- Another true/false format asks you to correct the false information so that a statement becomes true.

Rewrite to correct the mistakes below.

3. ___F___   The Mississippi River, which runs from east to west, empties into the Gulf of Mexico.

_____

4. ___F___   Climates near the equator tend to be extremely cold.

_____

Too Many Choices

- Analyze multiple-choice questions carefully.
- Understand the point and direction of the question.
- Predict the answer *before* looking at the answer choices.

Examine the questions below, cover the answer choices, predict the correct answer, and then eliminate as many answers as you can. Finally, fill in the bubble next to the answer that is the best choice.

1. Biology refers to the study of _____.

  (a) outer space   (d) human behavior

  (b) living things   (e) weather

  (c) rock formations

2. Which of the following movies is a Disney animated cartoon?

  (a) *Aladdin*   (d) *Batman*

  (b) *The Incredible Journey*   (e) *The Sound of Music*

  (c) *Star Wars*

- Some multiple-choice questions are written in reverse or backwards.

For instance, suppose question #1 above was written this way: *Which one of the things listed would NOT be studied in biology?* What would you do? You can't really predict the answer in the same way as you did before, but you can still think of the definition of *biology* before taking a peek at the answers. But now when you look at the answer choices, all of the answers will be things associated with the study of biology, except one. And that one will be the correct answer!

3. Which one of the things listed below would NOT be studied in biology?

  (a) the study of plants   (c) the study of kelp   (e) the study of planets

  (b) the study of cells   (d) the study of animals

4. Each one of the ancient deities listed below is female, except _____.

  (a) Hera   (c) Zeus   (e) Artemis

  (b) Aphrodite (d) Athena

Fill-in-the-Blanks!

You can plan ahead for fill-in-the-blank or completion test questions, just as you do for other types of test questions.

- DO some predicting when you study for a fill-in-the-blank test. Start by asking yourself, "What kinds of information would make good fill-in-the-blank questions—events, definitions, terms, or dates?"

- DO make flash cards for science or math tests, historical figures, vocabulary. Place the term or name on the front and the definition or event on the back.

- DO remember to read the test directions and mark the key words.

- DO remember to fill in every blank section of the test.

- DO remember that some fill-in-the-blank questions require one-word answers.

- DO remember that some tests may require a phrase rather than a one-word answer. Be sure you know what is expected. Ask questions if the directions are not clear.

Read the paragraph below carefully. Highlight important words, especially clue words. Then, review the words in the word bank and fill in the blank with the letter that best completes it. Cross out word bank items as you use them. Not all will be used. None will be used twice.

a. circus
b. peanut vendor
c. clown
d. acrobats
e. elephants
f. cyclists
g. lion tamer

When the _____ came to our small town, everyone rushed out to buy tickets. On the night of the big event, the townspeople filled the big top to capacity. The first to march in were the majestic _____ covered in gold brocade and bells, carrying their riders on their trunks. There was a swell of laughter as a _____ acted terrified of a tabby cat being led into the arena by the _____ who cracked his whip and waved his chair at the "dangerous" tabby. What a funny sight that was! Then came the _____, some perched high on unicycles and others roaring in on brightly polished motorcycles. Every costume was dazzling, especially the sequined outfits worn by the athletic _____ who piled on top of each other until a twelve-person pyramid had been formed!

Short Answer Tests

- Short and to the point—that's the key to your success when you're asked to write short answers in a test. Usually short-answer test questions measure your knowledge of specific information. You may be asked to list some information, or you may be asked to write a brief phrase. In some cases, you may be directed to write your answer in proper sentence form.

- The best study technique for short-answer tests is to review your notes, book, and study guides. Then, consider the information your teacher stressed in discussion and review. Develop the habit of predicting which information lends itself well to the short-answer for-mat. Make up short-answer questions, and answer them, too!

Read and analyze the two paragraphs above. Underline key words or phrases. Using that information, predict four short-answer questions that a teacher might ask you on a test about test-taking. Then answer the questions in the space provided. An example has been done for you.

Question example   *Briefly explain what short-answer questions measure.*

Answer example   _____*a student's knowledge of specific information*_____

1. Q. _____
   A. _____

2. Q. _____
   A. _____

3. Q. _____
   A. _____

4. Q. _____
   A. _____

Briefly explain how writing your own short-answer test could help your prepare for a real test.

_____

_____

Find the Purpose

Essay questions are designed to assess your ability to communicate your knowledge effectively at a higher level of thinking. Your teachers want to know whether you can evaluate and analyze the information you've learned. They want you to show the connections between different concepts and ideas.

• Find the purpose or goal of the question. Define what you are expected to prove or show.

To find out, circle the direction words. Direction words are words that tell you what to do. Then underline the key words that explain what you are to write. Key words are words that help explain the task.

Examples: A. (State) your opinion about raising the driving age to 18 years.

B. (Provide) three examples of evidence to support your opinion.

Read the essay questions below carefully. Circle (and number if needed) the direction words. Underline the key words that help you understand what you are to write.

1. Explain the meaning of the quote, "Give me liberty, or give me death." Explain who said it, when, and the circumstances under which it was said. Finally, describe the events that resulted from that remark.

2. Explain the meaning of "survival of the fittest" in the animal world. Describe what can happen when people interfere with the natural order of things in the animal world. Give two supporting examples.

3. What scientific evidence is there to support the idea that we are not the only intelligent life form in the universe? Based on the evidence, explain your opinion.

4. Explain the reasons England opposed the idea of independence for the thirteen American colonies. What happened as a result of their attitude?

5. Compare and contrast women's rights in 1900 with women's rights today. Compare and contrast at least two different areas of women's rights.

6. Humans need to become more responsible caretakers of the earth. Describe one program or law that is working today to meet this goal. Finally, if you could design a plan for making people and/or industry more responsible caretakers of our planet, what would that plan be?

Pre-writing Notes

For some essay tests, you must write a persuasive argument defending
your opinion on a specific topic. To write persuasively, you must organize
your ideas before starting to write. It takes only a minute or two, but a good essay depends on
this step. Use the margin of your test or a scrap piece of paper to jot down your ideas for
answering the essay question. This is called pre-writing.

Read the essay question below. Use the format below to help you pre-write your answer.

*Imagine that you could be any person in history for one day. Who would you be? Describe
three reasons why you would want to be this person. Finally, describe one act you would like to
do as this person.*

- Organize your thoughts. Start by answering the questions below. At first, don't worry about
  writing sentences or putting your thoughts in order.

- After writing your ideas, number them in the order you would use them in your essay.

Who would you be? _____

Describe your first reason for wanting to be this person.

_____

_____

Describe your second reason for wanting to be this person.

_____

_____

Describe your third reason for wanting to be this person.

_____

_____

Finally, describe one act you would like to accomplish as this person.

_____

_____

**On a separate sheet of paper, develop your
notes into an essay.**

FS30207 Test-Taking Skills

Write It Right!

Read the following essay question.

Describe a funny event that happened to a main character in a story that you have read.

Story _____ Character _____

On a separate sheet of paper, pre-write your answer to this question. Pre-write means jot down your ideas for answering.

Use the following guide to answer the essay question.

- First, write a brief opening or introductory paragraph based on your pre-writing notes. The first sentence states the topic. _____

  _____

  The second sentence expands the topic. _____

  _____

  The third sentence zeroes in on the focus or point of your answer. _____

  _____

- Next, write a body paragraph using your pre-writing notes. Include the explanation of the event, describing who, what, where, and when about the event.

  The first sentence gives specific information about the event. _____

  _____

  The next few sentences add detail or provide more support. _____

  _____

  _____

- The last paragraph is the concluding paragraph. In it, summarize the essay's key points. It is not necessary to add more facts or information in the conclusion, but it is a good idea to draw a conclusion or make a statement of evaluation.

  First, write the summary sentence. _____

  _____

  Then, write a sentence or two to make your conclusion or explanation. _____

  _____

Now, write your essay on another sheet of paper. Remember to proofread and edit your work!

Name _____

Standardized Test Answer Sheet

Use this answer sheet for the standardized tests following this page.

Use only a #2 pencil. Write the title of the test you are taking at the top of the page. Fill in the answer circles as completely and darkly as possible. If you change your answer, be sure to completely erase your first choice. Do not make any marks on this page besides your answers and the section title.

Test: _____

1. ⓐ ⓑ ⓒ ⓓ ⓔ

2. ⓐ ⓑ ⓒ ⓓ ⓔ

3. ⓐ ⓑ ⓒ ⓓ ⓔ

4. ⓐ ⓑ ⓒ ⓓ ⓔ

5. ⓐ ⓑ ⓒ ⓓ ⓔ

6. ⓐ ⓑ ⓒ ⓓ ⓔ

7. ⓐ ⓑ ⓒ ⓓ ⓔ

8. ⓐ ⓑ ⓒ ⓓ ⓔ

9. ⓐ ⓑ ⓒ ⓓ ⓔ

10. ⓐ ⓑ ⓒ ⓓ ⓔ

11. ⓐ ⓑ ⓒ ⓓ ⓔ

12. ⓐ ⓑ ⓒ ⓓ ⓔ

Teacher/Parent: Give each student a copy of this page for each section of the standardized test. These tests are on pages 20-31 in this book. You can also use it in conjunction with tests you write yourself.

FS30207 Test-Taking Skills

Read to Understand

- To identify the main idea of any reading passage, first read the passage. Then answer these questions which will make it easier to state the main idea clearly.

What/who is the passage about? _____

What happened? _____

When did it happen? _____

Where did it happen? _____

Why/how did it happen? _____

Read the passage below. Before you answer the comprehension questions that follow it, answer the questions above, about who, what, when, where, and why.

Reba wanted to star in the school play, but she couldn't predict what would happen at the audition. She stood in the wings, waiting and fretting. She began to feel queasy. Her stomach felt like a herd of stampeding elephants.

Reba wondered why she had longed for this moment. It wasn't magical like she'd expected. Yesterday she'd felt like a star and everything seemed possible. She was well prepared. She knew her lines. Today she could see she'd been a fool to listen to her family and friends. She wasn't as good as they said. Tears of defeat formed in the corners of her eyes. "I gotta get out of here," she said to no one, turning to walk away.

"I heard that! Don't you dare turn tail and run," an emphatic voice said sharply.

Reba whirled around in the direction of the voice, but she realized she was the only person left waiting in the wings. "Who...?"

"Well, Reba, are you ready? Then hustle, hustle, young lady. The show must go on, and all that jazz," said the drama coach impatiently from his perch in the orchestra pit.

It was too late to run. Ignoring the tears, she walked to the center stage and waited for her cue.

"Go for it, Reba!" said the emphatic voice. This time Reba recognized the voice as her courage speaking. She smiled.

Write the main idea of the story. _____

1. From the story, you can infer that

   _____ .

   (a) Reba's family supported her goal

   (b) Reba was one of the first to audition

   (c) Reba was a jazz musician trying out

   (d) Reba's audition took place after school

2. The best choice for the story's main idea is

   _____ .

   (a) Reba should have practiced more

   (b) Reba became nervous at the audition

   (c) Reba overcame her self-doubt

   (d) Reba's friends gave her an inflated opinion of her talent

Name _____

What's the Big Idea?

- Finding the main idea is a matter of collecting and sorting details so that you can understand the larger idea the author wanted to share with you.

Read the nonfiction article below. Then answer the questions.

Snowflake is the only known albino gorilla in the world. He was born about 1965 in the wild in the West African country of Equatorial Guinea. Taken captive as a youth, Snowflake has spent most of his life in the primate center at the zoo in Barcelona, Spain.

Snowflake's albinism happened before his birth while he was developing inside his mother's womb. It was not the result of heredity. Evidence that albinism is not hereditary can be taken from the fact that none of Snowflake's 21 offspring were albino. All were born with the normal black coloring of gorillas.

Snowflake is known for his albino features, including his pink face, hands, and feet. However, it is his albinism that caused his weak eyesight. In all other ways, Snowflake is a strong and healthy male at the age of thirty-two years. Perhaps, like some captive gorillas, Snowflake will continue to make children and adults "ooh" and "ahh" well into his fifth decade!

1. Albino refers to the lack of _____ .
   - (a) heredity
   - (b) good eyesight
   - (c) the ability to reproduce
   - (d) sufficient pigment in skin and fur

2. Snowflake has spent most of his life _____ .
   - (a) in Africa where he was born.
   - (b) touring with a circus.
   - (c) in a zoo in Spain.
   - (d) in a museum in Barcelona.

3. The sentence that best expresses the main idea of the article is _____ .
   - (a) albino gorillas breed well in captivity.
   - (b) albino gorillas live to be fifty.
   - (c) Snowflake is unique among the gorillas.
   - (d) Snowflake's children had normal color.

Drawing Conclusions

Any story presents you with a lot of information. As you read, you must pull the information together in a way so that you can draw a conclusion.

- To draw a conclusion, you must add up the known details to equal a new thought or idea. Often by previewing the questions first, you will know which details to add together.

Before you read the following passage, read the questions. See what kinds of information you'll need to "add up" to enable you to draw the correct conclusions. Then answer the questions.

Ito loved to draw. He drew all the time—at home, on the bus to school, and during lunch. Most of his drawings were caricatures of people, or the kind of drawing that exaggerates a person's features. Everyone at school enjoyed his sense of humor. Ito never used his caricatures to make fun of others. Ito carried several sketch books with him at all times. They were his greatest treasures.

1. From this selection, you can conclude that _____ .

    (a) Ito had few friends   (c) Ito liked to criticize others

    (b) Ito greatly valued his sketchbooks   (d) Ito didn't pay attention in class

Add up the known facts of the story to draw the conclusion.

Ito likes to draw. + He drew all the time. + He liked to draw caricatures. + People at school enjoyed his caricatures. + His sketchbooks were his greatest assets = There is nothing in the story that claims Ito was unpopular, critical, or distracted. Therefore **b** must be the right answer!.

Answer the rest of the questions about Ito and his drawings.

2. From this reading, you can conclude that _____ .

    (a) caricatures are meant to point out a person's ugly features

    (b) pets make better subjects for caricatures than people

    (c) caricatures require hours of detailed work to make them beautiful to the eye

    (d) caricatures are meant to make people laugh or smile

3. Which excerpt from the story best helps you conclude that Ito was a kind person?

    (a) Everyone at school enjoyed his humor and talent.

    (b) Ito liked to draw caricatures of people.

    (c) Ito's sketch books were his treasures.

    (d) Ito never used his caricatures to make fun of others.

    22   FS30207 Test-Taking Skills

Let's Have Order, Please!

In the reading comprehension section of a standardized test, you may be asked questions about the order in which the events occur.

- Watch for the *clue words*—words that indicate the passing of time or the order of things, such as:

  before, during, after, first, next, now, then, later, finally

- Notice *flashbacks* which carry the reader back to an earlier moment in the life of a character in the story, as in the following example:

Pele was eager for the race to begin. He glanced at his watch—two minutes to go. He stretched his long legs one more time. After checking his shoelaces, he took his place at the starting line and waited for the crack of the gun. His father's words suddenly echoed in his mind, "Pele, no matter what happens in the race this afternoon, you'll always be number one to me!" Pele scanned the crowd, but he couldn't see his father anywhere. Then came the starting shot, and Pele was off!

Read the passage above and underline the sentence that contains the flashback. Then circle any clue words that helped you understand the sequence of events. Next, number the events in the order in which they really occurred. Finally, answer the questions below.

1. When did Pele take his place at the starting line?
   - (a) after the race began
   - (b) after checking his shoelaces
   - (c) before checking the time
   - (d) after looking for his father

2. When did Pele's father speak to him?
   - (a) at dinner the night before the race
   - (b) after Pele ran the race
   - (c) just before Pele's warm-up stretches
   - (d) on the morning of the race

3. When did Pele recall his father's words?
   - (a) as soon as he got into position to run
   - (b) while he was doing warm-up stretches
   - (c) after he looked to find his dad in the crowd
   - (d) just after he checked his watch

Context Clues

Frequently in standardized tests, you will be asked questions about the meanings of words. Some are vocabulary words that you are expected to know. But some may be unfamiliar words whose meanings can be understood based on the context of the sentence and passage in which they appear. Try the strategies below for figuring out the meaning of an unfamiliar word.

- Look for clues to the unfamiliar word's meaning from other words and phrases in the sentence or the paragraph.

- When you do find a word or phrase that seems to mean the same, put it in the unfamiliar word's place.

- Predict your answer **before** looking at the answer choices!

Select the word that is closest in meaning to the word in bold type.

1. The building was empty when the manager locked her office for the night. In the stillness, her footsteps **reverberated** down the long, empty corridor, echoing like hollow ping pong balls.

    ⓐ walked   ⓑ hurried   ⓒ ran   ⓓ echoed

Select the antonym to the highlighted word. Antonyms are opposite in meaning.

2. Because he was a **diligent** student, Luke always worked hard on every project.

    ⓐ inconsiderate   ⓑ studious   ⓒ lazy   ⓓ clever

Select a synonym for the highlighted word. Synonyms have similar meanings.

3. It's not emotionally healthy to **harbor** bad feelings. Holding ill will inside can damage a friendship.

    ⓐ hold   ⓑ let go   ⓒ give   ⓓ resent

Select the best word to complete the sentence.

4. Following the concert, the audience rose to its feet and shouted, "_____ !"

    ⓐ Bravo   ⓑ Welcome   ⓒ Oh no   ⓓ Hello

The Art of Language

One section of a standardized test may be devoted to language arts.
This test section is designed to assess your ability to correctly spell,
capitalize, punctuate, and to find mistakes in usage. Additionally, you
may be assessed on your ability to edit and revise sentences from short
reading passages. Practice using some of the different test formats used in the language arts
section of a standardized test.

Select the word from the list below that is NOT spelled correctly.

1. (a) principol   (b) ordinary   (c) primary   (d) no errors

**Select the line that includes a spelling error. Some lines have no errors. If there are no
spelling errors, then select the last answer.**

2. (a) Tyler stayed after school to rehearse

    (b) his solo peace on the trumpet. He

    (c) almost missed the late bus.

    (d) no error

**Select the line that has an error in capitalization. If there is no error,
select the last answer.**

3. (a) "I wonder," Ulee thought, "If

    (b) Corinne remembered to bring

    (c) her journal to english class."

    (d) no errors

Select the line that has an error in grammar usage.

4. (a) One student with the highest math

    (b) scores is receiving an award at the

    (c) assembly. Since the new girls grades

    (d) are the best, she'll get the award.

Edit, Revise, and Rewrite!

Standardized tests are likely to have whole sections devoted to assessing your ability to edit, revise, and rewrite. The formats may vary from test to test, or even within the same test.

(1) Where robots once were superstars of science fiction movies, they are now becoming superstars of the operating room. (2) Scientists are currently working on one such robot that will be used in hip replacement surgery. (3) It is called ROBODOC. (4) Its job will be to drill the hole in the bone. (5) Then its human partner, an orthopedic surgeon will set the implant in place.

1. **Select the sentence that best combines sentences (3) and (4) from the article into one.**

   (a) Its human partner will set the implant in place and the robot will drill the hole.

   (b) One such science-fiction robot, performing an important task, will be used in hip replacement surgery.

   (c) Called ROBODOC, its job will be to drill the hole in the bone.

   (d) Although it is called ROBODOC, its job will be to drill the hole in the bone.

2. **Select the sentence that is the best way to correct the mistake in sentence (5).**

   (a) Then it's human partner, the orthopedic partner will set the implant in place.

   (b) Then its human partner an orthopedic surgeon will set the implant in place.

   (c) Then its human partner, an orthopedic surgeon, will set the implant in place.

   (d) Then its human partner and the orthopedic surgeon will set the implant in place.

3. **Select the sentence that best concludes the paragraph on robots.**

   (a) Fortunately for the patient, he or she will be asleep during the operation.

   (b) But not before he has lots of practice.

   (c) Within the next ten years, scientists will have a cure for hip disease.

   (d) Scientists are hopeful that ROBODOC will assist in operations soon.

Read and Edit, Too!

Because not all standardized tests follow exactly the same pattern, it's a good idea for you to be familiar with different test designs. Some combine the language arts and reading sections.

- Begin by reading all the directions.

Read the entire passage before answering any questions. Then look at each underlined part to decide what needs to be changed. Select the best answer. Choose "no mistake" if no change is needed.

If you are **(1)** <u>curios</u> about strange science facts, you'll like reading this article about electrophotography, or what is also known as Kirlian photography. Semyon and Valentina Kirlian were thought to be the creators of this process. **(2)** However, <u>it turns out that</u> like many other **(3)** <u>scientists in history she developed</u> the process by modifying someone else's idea. In the 1700's, Georg Lichtenberg was the first to produce the ring or corona that **(4)** <u>circles a electrically-charged object</u>. The eerie, outlined shape that resulted was called a "Lichtenberg" figure.

1. (a) corious
    (b) curious
    (c) curous
    (d) no mistake

2. (a) It turned out, that,
    (b) It turns out, however,
    (c) It turned out however;
    (d) no mistake

3. (a) scientists, in history, she developed
    (b) scientists in history they developed
    (c) scientists in history, they developed
    (d) no mistake

4. (a) circles an electrically-charged object.
    (b) circle a electrically-charged object.
    (c) circles a electrically-charged object.
    (d) no mistake

FS30207 Test-Taking Skills

Name _____

Read, Edit, Go!

Read the entire passage before answering or rewriting the questions. Look at each underlined part to decide what needs to be changed. Select the best answer. Choose "no mistake" only if you are sure that no change is needed.

It wasn't until the late (1) <u>1930's. The Kirlian's changed Lichtenberg's</u> method of creating a corona around an electrically-charged object. Unlike Lichtenberg, who used scattered dust to create the corona, the Kirlians used camera film to capture the corona around a charged object. (2) <u>How did they do it</u>. First, they gave an electric jolt to ordinary objects like (3) <u>leaves and twigs and keys and coins</u>. Then they photographed the colorful discharge of energy from the objects.

1. (a) 1930's that the Kirlians changed Lichtenberg's
    (b) 1930's when the Kirlian's changed Lichtenberg's
    (c) 1930's that the Kirlian's changed Lichtenbergs
    (d) no mistakes

2. (a) How did they do it!
    (b) How, did they do it?
    (c) How did they do it?
    (d) no mistake

3. (a) leaves and twigs, and keys and coins.
    (b) leaves, twigs, keys, and coins.
    (c) leaves twigs keys and coins.
    (d) no mistake

The Kirlians later caused a controversy among scientists. When they said that the corona around living things could be used to diagnose disease—even those diseases without symptoms! Today's metallurgists use electrophotography to test the quality of weld joints in metals, not the bone joints in humans with aches and pains.

4. From this article, you can infer that _____ .
    (a) electrophotography is a hoax
    (b) scientists sometimes build upon the ideas of others
    (c) it was proven that Kirlian photography could diagnose disease
    (d) the Kirlians were Lichtenberg's friends

It Adds Up to Excellence

Math is included in standardized tests, generally in multiple-choice format. The questions often combine different kinds of questions to assess your mastery of basic math concepts, operations, and problem-solving techniques appropriate for your grade level. The problems cover all areas of interest, including other subject areas and real world problems.

Read the passage below. Select the best answers.

At Clamer Middle School, Mr. Bergman announced to his class on Monday that they would take a standardized math test in seven days. The students asked lots of questions about what to expect in the test. After discussion, the students said they would like to prepare a practice test so that they could review. Mr. Bergman agreed. The class then divided into nine teams. Each team made up a section of questions for one type of skill or concept. The chart shows the results of their work.

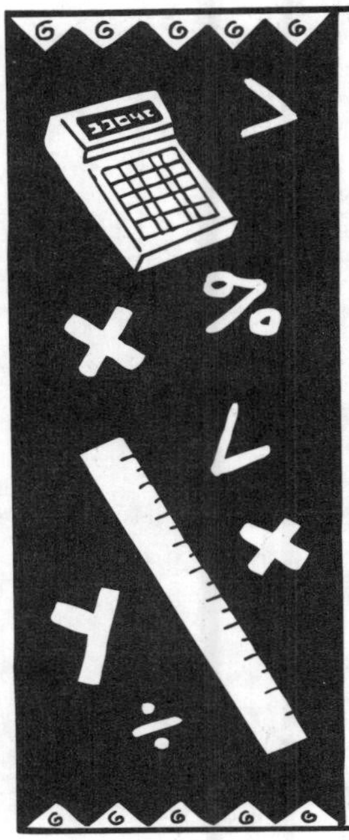

A Practice Math Test

Question Type	Amount of Each
percent	6 percent
place value	3 percent
geometry	10 percent
measurement	10 percent
estimation	5 percent
decimals	15 percent
fractions	8 percent
calculation	15 percent
problem solving	?

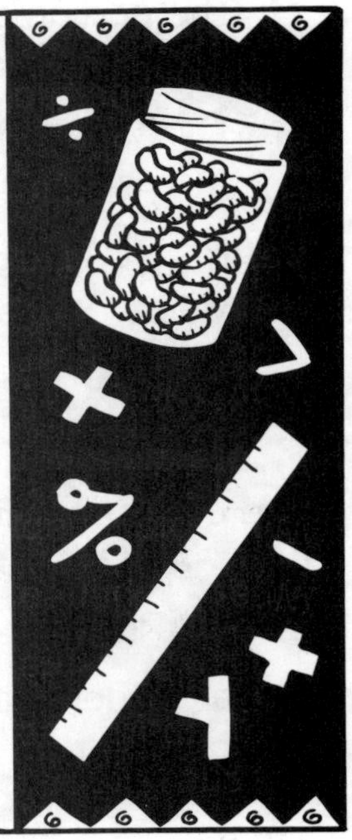

1. On what day will Mr. Bergman's students be taking the standardized test?

   ⓐ Monday, a week later   ⓑ Sunday ⓒ Tuesday   ⓓ none of these

2. Estimate the percentage of the test that reviewed problem solving skills.

   ⓐ 70% ⓑ 72% ⓒ 60%   ⓓ none of these

3. Which two practice test sections equalled exactly eleven percent?

   ⓐ fractions and place value   ⓒ percent and estimation
   ⓑ fractions and estimation   ⓓ both **a** and **c**

Reading Math

Read the passage below. Then answer the questions that follow using the information from the following paragraph.

Have you noticed what our local students are doing in school these days? Take a walk to the once shabby playground at the corner of Elm Street and Warren Way, and you'll be amazed to see Mr. Santo's twenty-five math students there. For two hours every day for twenty days, Mr. Santo's class has worked after school to design and build a math project called the Geometry Playground. The playground is not like any other. In fact, it's more like a three-dimensional sculpture than a playground. Giant 3-D geometric shapes made of strong pieces of rubber and plastic cover the playground. Where once only weeds grew, now there are children running, jumping, climbing, and playing!

The area of a region is the number of square units needed to cover the region.

1. The portion of the playground covered by giant red cubes measures 20 feet long by 15 feet wide. What is its area?

    (a) 35 sq. ft.   (b) 5 sq. ft.   (c) 300 sq. ft.   (d) 250 sq. ft.

2. The park has a section devoted to tall shapes for children to climb. This section is 38 feet wide by 11 feet long. Estimate its area.

    (a) 50 sq. ft.   (b) 400 sq. ft.   (c) 372 sq. ft.   (d) 300 sq. ft.

The cost of building the playground was $12,000 dollars. The city council paid 60% of the costs, and the students raised the rest through bake sales, a read-a-thon, and a car wash.

3. The largest single sum of money came from the

    (a) student bake sales   (c) student car wash

    (b) student read-a-thon   (d) city council

4. What percent of the cost of building the playground

    came from student sources?

    (a) 30%   (b) 50%   (c) 25%   (d) 40%

Graphic Math

Graphs and Charts

Illustrations, graphs, charts, and maps are often used in standardized tests to help students understand information in a visual way.

- Carefully read the words and data on the map, chart, or graph before answering the questions. Then, as you begin to solve the problem, ask yourself:

— "What do I already know?"

— "What is it that I need to find out?"

— "What process(es) or operation(s) will help me solve the problem?"

— "Does my answer make sense?"

Read the passage below. Then answer the questions that follow using the information from the following paragraph.

The pupils in Ms. Drobsky's class surveyed many students to gather data about career interests. But this was no ordinary survey, because they used the computer to e-mail students in other schools all around the state. Ms. Drobsky's class was able to graph the careers that topped the list of student favorites.

each **X** represents 50 students	**Four Careers Students Most Want**
doctor	X X X X X X X X X X X X X X X X X X X X X
teacher	X X X X X X X X X X X X X
engineer	X X X X X X X X X X
lawyer	X X X X X X X X X

1. To find out the number of students who were surveyed, you would

   (a) Add all the symbols and then divide by fifty

   (b) Add all the symbols and subtract fifty

   (c) Divide fifty by four

   (d) Add all the symbols and multiply by fifty

2. What is the total number of students surveyed by Ms. Drobsky's class?

   (a) 2,200   (b) 2,650   (c) 2,570   (d) 2,602

3. The sum of which two careers equals 1,150 students?

   (a) engineer and doctor   (c) teacher and doctor

   (b) teacher and engineer   (d) engineer and lawyer

Answers

Page 3
Highlighting of text will vary.
1. Limestone peaks rose from the sea millions of years ago.
2. The river provides transportation as well as water for farming and fish for food.
3. People work and live with the river and the earth.

Page 8
Time Allotment: Answers will vary but must total no more than 40 minutes.

Underlined words:

Math Read problem; Write name process; solve problem; show work; circle solution

Science Select two constellations; draw them; explain legend of one name

History Read; write T or F; rewrite false statement

Reading Read; select answer main idea; record answers.

Page 10
1. d
2. e
3. a
4. b
5. c
6. i
7. h
8. f
9. g

Page 11
1. F - always
2. F - all
3. T - most
4. F - always
5. F - most
6. T - many
7. F - all

Page 12
1. T ~~not impossible~~
   During severe tornados, it is possible for . . .
2. T ~~not unknown~~
   Excellent athletes were known...
3. The Mississippi River runs north to south.
4. Climates near the equator tend to be hot. OR Climates near the poles tend to be extremely cold.

Page 13
1. b
2. a
3. e
4. c

Page 14
Answers in order are:
a - e - c - g - f - d

Page 16
1. Circled: explain, explain, describe
   Underlined: who, when, circumstances, events
2. Circled: explain, describe, give
   Underlined: meaning, what, two examples
3. Circled: explain.
   Underlined: what, to support the idea, not the only
4. Circled: explain
   Underlined: the reasons, what happened
5. Circled: compare and contrast.
   Underlined: 1900, today, two different areas
6. Circled: describe, design.
   Underlined: one program or law, a plan, what

Page 20
Main Idea: Reba lost her confidence at the audition until her inner voice restored her self-confidence.
1. a
2. c

Page 21
1. d
2. c
3. c

Page 22
2. d
3. d

Page 23
Flashback sentence: His father's words suddenly echoed in his mind, "Pele, no matter...you'll always be number one to me."

Clue words: after, then

Sequence of events: 1) Pele's father offered words of encouragement 2) checked his watch 3) stretched legs 4) checked his laces 5) took his place 6) scanned the crowd 7) starting shot 8) Pele was off
1. b
2. d
3. a

Page 24
1. d
2. c
3. a
4. a

Page 25
1. a (principal)
2. b (piece)
3. c (English)
4. c (girl's)

Page 26
1. c
2. c
3. d

Page 27
1. b
2. d
3. c
4. a

Page 28
1. a
2. c
3. b
4. b

Page 29
1. a
2. d
3. d

Page 30
1. c
2. b
3. d
4. d

Page 31
1. d
2. b
3. b